Solange Kergreis

SMALL GIFTS

IN FRENCH *Trapunto*

Kangaroo Press

Preface

For lovers of the art of French trapunto I have chosen a number of small items that can be quickly made under skilful fingers, whether you be a veteran or novice of this art form. They make beautiful and charming gifts and despite their apparent simplicity each piece constitutes a tiny work of art.

The sumptuousness of the antique French trapunto marriage quilts and bridal skirts so admired in museums and antique shops can make the observer's imagination reel. How much more then, does *involvement* in the art, the realisation, stitch by stitch, of even a more humble piece, make women today the inheritors of that feminine knowledge from past centuries? This is a knowledge which is transmitted from generation to generation, carrying with it all the warmth, sensuality and authenticity of an earlier time.

Such objects become a part of you and your loved ones' lives; they reflect your dreams and hopes, your patience and your skill, and your passion for things of beauty to those who know how to listen!

A note on technique

Interior decorating magazines which specialise in the antique art and furniture of Provence often fail to distinguish between the white padded embroidery known as *le boutis* (French trapunto) and other forms of quilting. Photographs of Marseilles quilting are often wrongly featured as trapunto. Marseilles quilting is composed of three layers of fabric (printed cretonne on top, thick flannel beneath and a lining fabric on the bottom layer). These layers are joined by a running stitch that follows a fairly simple design (cross bars or a plaited pattern). This is quite different from the technique described in my books.

A simple method of distinguishing between the two is to place the disputed piece against a window or other source of light. A quilted cover (which has a flannel layer between the two outer layers) cannot be seen through. A piece worked in the French trapunto style, on the other hand, will inevitably reveal gaps where the stitches are, translucent sections where there is no wadding.

Don't let yourself be deceived! A trapunto piece the size of a bedcover is much more rarely found than a simple quilted one, because it was so much more difficult to produce.

Antique embroideries from the collection of
Martine Manuel de Tournus

In France, quilted fabrics from Marseilles are mentioned as early as the thirteenth century in local inventories, listed as vannes *or* courtepointes *(display quilts and bedcovers). The production of articles of good quality depended on the sisterhood of the embroiderers, whom we know little about through the lack of surviving examples. It is thought, however, that the works of the fourteenth century were probably influenced by the quilted fabrics of the time from Palermo (the capital of Sicily), with which we are more familiar. A famous example of Sicilian quilting is the celebrated Tristan Quilt conserved in London's Victoria and Albert Museum.*

The Tristan quilt is quite fascinating. Unlike the quilts of Marseilles, which were made of cotton, the Tristan quilt was fashioned in linen and stuffed with wool rather than tiny wads of silk or cotton. This monumental work was bought in 1904 by the South Kensington Museum in London (now known as the Victoria and Albert Museum).

The upper layer of the quilt is made of a cream linen fabric and the underneath of a more rustic material. The centre of the quilt features six symmetrically arranged framed scenes, and there are eight scenes along the border, placed horizontally on the lower edge and vertically on the long sides. This assemblage calls to mind the system of bands and borders used by modern quilters.

The cartouches, wadded in relief in the French trapunto manner, are decorated with human figures and descriptive text in Sicilian dialect and Gothic characters and tell the legend of Tristan and Isolde.

The figures and the letters are worked in backstitch with a light brown thread that contrasts nicely with the fabric, with background patterning enhancing the pictures with marvellous stitching.

From an artistic point of view, the style of the scenes is fairly primitive but the tiny stitched faces are remarkably expressive. The gestures of the figures and the deliberately disproportionate size of their hands also clarify the story. From scene to scene there are large differences in the quality of the design and the stitchery, which suggests that the quilt was a collective project.

A quilt supposed to be the sister quilt of the Tristan quilt was discovered in Italy in the 1890s by the Countess Maddalena, who found it in the Guicciardini family residence at Usella near Prato. Staff on the property had been using it as a bedcover. This quilt also is composed of cartouches telling the story of Tristan and Isolde, but unlike the quilt in London, it is asymmetrical, suggesting that it was uncompleted.

The Countess, intrigued by the scenes and legends represented on the quilt, took it to an expert in Florence where she discovered its significance. The quilt was brought back to Usella and henceforth treated with the care warranted by its precious heritage.

In 1910 the Victoria and Albert Museum tried in vain to acquire it; in 1927 it was sold to the Museum of Bargello, a medieval fortress converted into a museum of sculpture. An inventory note telling of the acquisition of the quilt gives the following brief description:

Cover in white linen, embroidered with eight scenes in relief, following the history of Tristan with a descriptive text in Sicilian dialect and Gothic characters. It is composed of three longitudinal assembled bands and measures 2.41 m [95"] in height and 2.07 m [81½"] in width. Acquired for 90 000 lira in July 1927 from Count Paolo Guicciardini.

There is no doubt that the quilts of Usella and London constitute a pair because they share the same subjects, methods of construction and coat of arms carved on the shields (the family arms of Guicciardini).

The Breton story of the love between Tristan and Isolde, made famous in the legends of King Arthur, exists in many forms. The scenes portrayed on the two quilts record the events relating to the oppression of the Cornouille by the King of Ireland and his ally Amoroldo, and the struggle by Tristan on behalf of his uncle, King Mark.

It might seem strange that the embroiderers of Sicily should have chosen as their theme one of the legends of King Arthur, but in fact chivalric history has long had a place in Sicilian culture. According to the legend, the tombs of Tristan and Isolde are decorated with ivy and vine branches that intertwine as they grow. Hidden amongst the leaves decorating these wonderful quilts one can find these two plants tangled together.

We know that a marriage took place in 1395 between Laodomia Acialnoli and Piero di Luigi Guicciardini. It is probable that these quilts were sewn to celebrate the union of the two families, the eternal love which united Tristan and Isolde summoning the love which would unite the two betrothed.

Antique works lent by Boutique Fanette, 1 rue d'Alençon, 75015 Paris

Materials and techniques

French trapunto embroidery was traditionally produced on a plain white fabric. For the charm and brilliance of sparkling white, you are advised to use a fabric with a very fine weave for the top side of your work (cotton percale is most appropriate). However, there is nothing to prevent you from using fabric with an indigo blue or golden yellow hue, for subtlety and originality. However, always choose a plain cloth because on a printed fabric the motif would be confused with the patterning on the cloth and would lose its impact.

Materials

❀ Fabric a little larger than the size envisaged for your completed work (the wadding will reduce the total surface quite considerably).

❀ White, loosely woven fabric (e.g. calico) for the lining. The fibres of this chosen fabric must be able to be easily parted and then realigned to permit the completion of a piece as beautiful, or nearly as beautiful, on the reverse as on the front. Contrary to the rules for patchwork don't, under any circumstances, wash the fabric before commencing your work—you only need to wash the work once it's entirely finished. The washing, as well as tightening the fibres, will erase the tiny puncture holes left by inserting the wadding, wash away any traces of pencil, and will absorb any possible distortions created by the wadding.

❀ A fairly short quilting needle, no. 8 or no. 10 (see stores which specialise in patchwork supplies).

❀ A tapestry needle with a rounded tip.

❀ Sewing thread (white cotton).

❀ Small orange stick (from the manicure section in your local pharmacy). Rub it gently with fine sandpaper to smooth it down and refine the end.

❀ A washaway pencil to reproduce the motif.

❀ A large 60 cm (24″) ruler.

❀ Embroidery scissors.

❀ A small rubber needle puller with which to catch the needle as it comes through the fabric (see stores specialising in patchwork supplies).

Stuffing

It is preferable to use soft thick synthetic flannel for important sections of the motif such as the leaves or flower petals, and strong cotton candlewicking or thick yarn for the long narrow parts such as stems, scrolls, borders, parallel lines.

Method

Draw a 1 cm (³/₈″) border around the fabric with a fine pencil line (fig. 1); if you plan to create a panel with a central motif and a design in the corners, map out connecting lines from the centre of each side to obtain the triangles (fig. 2).

Next, fold your fabric in two lengthwise, then across the width, marking each fold line strongly with your fingernail. This guide will serve to centre your main motif (fig. 3).

If you are creating the border of a tablecloth, carrying a repeating motif, divide the border first into equal sections the size of the chosen motif with fine pencil lines. Mark the centre of each section by the fingernail method and reproduce your design in each one.

Now place your pattern under the fabric, matching its centre to the marked centre of the fabric. Trace all the outlines (you will be able to see the pattern through the fabric) using the washaway pencil.

Fig. 1

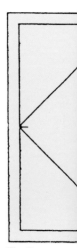

Fig. 2

Place the motif to be copied on a glass surface lit from behind by a lamp

Place the upper fabric over the motif and fix with tape

Trace the motif

Draw in the parallel lines of the infill at 5 mm (³/₁₆") intervals

In the case of a symmetrical pattern, start by drawing the quarter or the half according to the proposed pattern, then reproduce it symmetrically by pivoting or reversing the design.

Normally you can clearly see the outlines of the motif on the paper through white fabric. If, however, your fabric proves a little too thick and poses some transparency problems, you could tape the pattern to a window, fix the fabric over it with more tape, and trace the pattern. Alternatively, you could place the work over a sheet of transparent glass lit from below by a lamp. You could also use a light box.

To make the characteristic infill of parallel lines, draw parallel lines 5 mm (³/₁₆") apart, starting from one of the corners, along a single axis over the whole surface of the central square, except of course over the motif (see fig. 4 on the next page), or on two axes diverging from the midline (see fig. 5 on the next page). At the same time, map out, if necessary, 5 mm (³/₁₆") spaced diagonals in the triangles at the corners.

To make the job easier, mark the start of each line in lead pencil all around the perimeter of your work, marking each fifth point with a slightly longer pencil mark in the outer edge. It's advisable to draw the diagonals moving down the fabric, keeping the lines you've just drawn above the ruler to avoid slip-ups.

Once you've drawn the motif on the upper layer of fabric, place it onto the backing cloth, matching up the corners. Sew around the pencil border that you initially drew in a loose tacking stitch to hold the two layers together. Sew along the quarter lines and diagonals, delineating any corner triangles. Always start from the centre of the work, using a tacking stitch (fig. 6). Your work is ready to embroider.

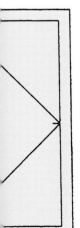
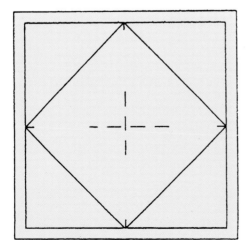

Fig. 3

Thread an embroidery needle with a small length of white thread, at the end of which you've tied a small reef knot (not a rolled knot). Starting on the right side of the fabric, take your needle through the two layers of fabric about 2 cm (¾") away from the motif. Bring the needle out at the line of the motif itself (fig. 7) and give the thread a sharp tug to make the knot disappear.

If you know how to quilt with a quilting frame, use it, ensuring that when you position the fabric you do not overstretch it. Pat the fabric with the flat of your hand to determine whether it has enough give to allow the stitches to pass through without effort.

Place your left hand under the frame, resting a finger (index or middle, depending on your preference), in the exact spot you wish to push the needle through, so that you can feel that it has passed through the two layers. (Yes, to begin with you'll prick yourself sometimes but over time a callus will form and you'll no longer feel the needle!)

Commence embroidering the central motif with a tiny regular running stitch. Embroider each section of the motif separately. Don't go over from one petal of a flower to another,

for example, even if they touch. When you've embroidered each section of the design, which will later be stuffed separately, catch the thread by forming a small reef knot which will later be hidden between the two layers of fabric. This method prevents the fabric buckling during the wadding of the work. Thus, even if you pull the thread a little too hard while padding a section, the section alongside will not pucker.

An alternative method involves making a strong tying off stitch at the end of each segment of the motif, then starting up again at the following part of the motif, slipping the needle through the two layers of the fabric. It's quicker, but a little more obvious.

When you've finished setting the motif, embroider the straight diagonal lines, using small running stitches, starting with the lines that touch the central motif and moving out towards the edge of the fabric. It's vital not to commence stitching in the corner and work towards the middle, because you risk finding yourself with a 'bubble' of fabric, which proves impossible to absorb, between the final diagonal and the edge of the design.

Fig. 4

Fig. 5

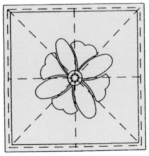

Fig. 6

Fig. 7

Padding

When you've finished quilting your work, you can commence padding it to give it the required relief.

Turn your work the wrong way up. At the base of each motif, with the aid of a well tapered orange stick, separate, without breaking, the threads of the loosely woven backing material. Work cautiously, taking care not to pierce the fine fabric of the top layer.

Place the middle finger of your left hand underneath your work, at the point at which you plan to enter with the orange stick, ensuring that it doesn't pierce the top fabric. Between the two layers of fabric, through the small hole you have

made, push a small piece of padding material. Roll one end of each little piece to more easily insert it.

Turn the orange stick gently as you push the padding through. You will find a large tapestry needle useful for pushing the padding through to the end of any particularly narrow motifs.

The padded motif should retain some degree of flexibility while having the maximum relief.

When the motif is padded to your satisfaction, close the little holes left by the orange stick, and reposition the threads with the point of the needle.

Padding stems, diagonals and fine lines

Thread your needle with a length of yarn, single or doubled depending on its thickness. Again from the back, pass the thread between the two lines of stitching delineating a stem or a diagonal. If the section to be put into relief presents a strong curve, for instance the circumference of a heart (fig. 8), enter the needle at point A, then make it exit the fabric at the maximum level of curvature—point B. Pull on the thread, leaving a good 1 cm ($^3/_8$") protruding at A. If you pull a little too strongly, you risk making the yarn disappear into the 'tunnel' (thereby leaving a small portion not padded). Now take the needle again into the exact same hole B and slip it gently towards the end of the line to wad in successive stages—C, D and E. Pull again on the thread to make the loops formed at the holes disappear, and then cut the cotton with embroidery scissors level with the entry and exit points.

Draw out the work between your two hands, with little sharp tugs, to make the 'wicks' of cotton completely disappear.

When the element you are stuffing starts or finishes with an angled edge, make the needle enter and leave at the most distant points so that you don't leave the tips empty (fig. 9).

Remember to conceal all the holes left by the path of the needle by drawing the threads back together with the point of a fine needle.

When all the stuffing is done, finish the work with a bias edging made from the fine upper surface fabric. Wash the piece with a small amount of washing powder, then with a product to whiten the cotton. Dry it flat on terry towelling, pinning it out to shape with strong pins.

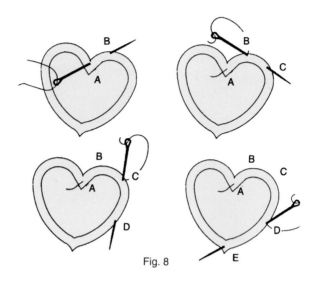

Fig. 8

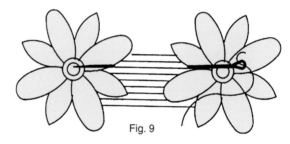

Fig. 9

Finishing touches

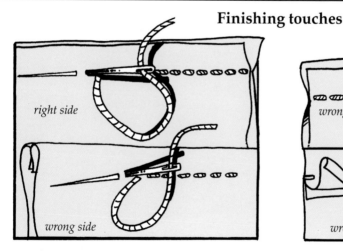

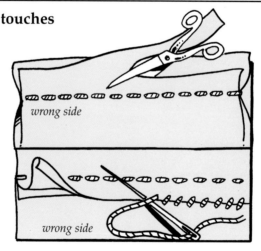

French seam

Sew with wrong sides of the fabric together. Turn over and flatten the seam with a fingernail or press with an iron. Close the edges of first seam with a second seam, with the right sides of the fabric together.

Run and fell seam

Make a first line of stitching with the right sides of the fabric together. Cut one of the sides. Fold down over the other side. Hold down with overstitch, turning under the raw edge.

Handy hints

For quilting use a good brand of strong white thread which isn't going to break during the stuffing. As you do the stitching, make sure that each stitch passes through both layers of material and that the motif appears as clear on the back of your work as on the front.

Sometimes a finely pointed element of a motif (a leaf or petal, for example) will appear a little flat. You can stick a fine pin into the padded element and use it to 'persuade' the stuffing into the tip. Again, draw the threads together to conceal any hole.

To finish off your work, if necessary, quilt with a tapestry needle into the centre of the motif, taking it out at the furthest point. Slide the cotton until it disappears completely into the small hole left by the needle. Cut the other end with embroidery scissors level with the point. Reclose the hole.

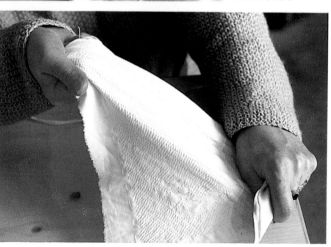

1. Materials for padding.
2. Insert the round tipped needle into the back of the work.
3. Slide the needle to the end of the section, gathering the fabric.
4. Use a needle puller to hold the tip of the needle.
5. Cut the thread level with the fabric at both ends.
6. Pull the fabric between your hands to hide the end of the thread inside the 'tunnel'.

Waterlilies

Purse

*F*or those important occasions such as weddings and baptisms this elegant and delicatel evening purse can be used in place of a handbag to hold your little knick-knacks—cosmetics to touch up your makeup or tissues to wipe away your tears of emotion!

Requirements

❀ 40 cm (16") of very beautiful plain coloured, closely woven fabric (e.g. baptiste)

❀ Large white press stud

❀ Reel of white quilting thread

❀ Few snippets of white flannel

❀ White cotton yarn

Method

Cut the fabric into two equal pieces. Divide the piece that will form the outer part of your purse into three equal sections, using a light pencil line (see diagram). On the first section, draw in your waterlily motif. Map out the parallel line infill over the entire work, leaving 2 cm (¾") of fabric clear around the edges. Tack together the upper fabric and the lower layer, then sew together in running stitch before wadding the work as described on pages 6–11.

37.5 cm (14¾")

1

2

3

25.5 cm (10")

1/2 pattern
ACTUAL SIZE

Assemble your bag using a French seam. For this technique place the stuffed pieces one on top of the other (wrong sides together), and sew.

Turn the purse inside out now, flatten the seam with a fingernail, and then close the edges of the first seam with a second seam, right sides together. This technique leaves an impeccable finish on both the outside and the interior of the purse.

Place a bias strip of white satin around the edge, and finish by sewing the press-stud under the flap.

Comet's tail

Lingerie bag

The motif on this lingerie bag brings to mind the recent visits to our heavens of luminous comets, with the crystals of ice in their tails sparkling behind them. As beautiful as it is practical, this bag can be used to store outfits for a baby or fine linen for those weekends away. An asset to any hope chest, this piece will be one of the highlights of your work in French trapunto, reflecting your ability to transform utilitarian articles into accessories of beauty and charm.

Method

The bag is crafted in fine unbleached linen with the front carrying the comet motif. The back of the bag (cut it the same size as the front) is patterned only with parallel lines. Leave a good 2 cm (¾") of unworked fabric around each piece for making up. When you quilt the back and the front using a small running stitch, leave a 1 cm (³/₈") wide section unworked about 4 cm (1½") down from the top edge. Through this you will later run a drawstring to close the bag.

When you've finished the trapunto work, join the two pieces, wrong sides together, with machine stitch about 1 cm (³/₈") inside the edge. Turn the bag inside out, and flatten the seam with your fingernail. Close the edges of the first seam with a second seam (right sides of the fabric together). This method is called French seaming, and gives a clean finish to your work (see page 9).

Finish with a hand-stitched hem around the top, taking it to the very edge of the parallel lines of cording, and slip a small drawstring plaited with embroidery yarn through the space left for it.

1/2 pattern
ACTUAL SIZE

14

Oriental brooch

Lingerie bag

ere's another small lingerie bag, this time made in a fine white cotton fabric. The motif was inspired by a fibula, the jewelled brooch which Oriental women use to secure the drapes of their costume. Make this bag following the method described on page 14.

1/2 pattern
ACTUAL SIZE

Daisies

This work is as light as a breath of air that ripples through the wild meadow daisies, drowsing in the gentle summer sun. It is also an extremely useful piece of work. Despite its delicate appearance, you need not be afraid of using this potholder in the kitchen, because it is washable and dries flat, without needing to be ironed.

Edge the potholder with a fairly wide line through which you pass eight lengths of cotton yarn. Finish with a small loop of white plaited or buttonholed cotton, folded in two, sewn into one corner so you can easily hang your new treasure.

ACTUAL SIZE

18

Christmas Rose and Mexican Creeper

Napkin rings

Attractively embroidered in trapunto using distinctive original patterns, these unique napkin rings look beautiful wound around fine damask linen serviettes. Alternatively, use them with vibrantly coloured cotton napkins, which will show off the dazzling white of the trapunto pieces to great advantage.

Method

Work the trapunto quilting in the regular way. Finish the edges of the serviette rings with a run and fell seam (see sketch and explanation for this on page 9).

Mexican Creeper

ACTUAL SIZE

Christmas Rose

Finishing touches

Cover a small button with a small piece of the fine upper surface fabric, and sew it to the pointed end of the Christmas Rose napkin ring. On the opposite end make a buttonholed loop of fairly thick perle cotton for a clasp.

The Mexican Creeper napkin ring has a 30 cm (12") cord of twisted silk sewn at each end. Dip the ends of the cord in clear nail polish to prevent it unravelling.

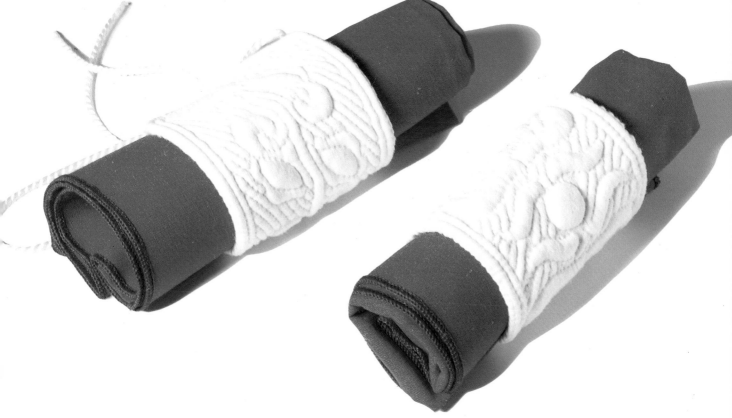

Marigold

Afternoon tea napkin

This lovely serviette is quick to make and adds to the ambiance when you're sampling varieties of tea—green, black or smoked—with the delicate aromas wafting from the kettle. Brightening up an old wooden tea tray discovered at a secondhand shop is easily done with this trapunto piece. A teapot of fine English china and a plate of buttered scones complete a pretty combination—you're ready to indulge in the time honoured tradition of afternoon tea.

ACTUAL SIZE

Method

Draw onto your fabric a 19 cm (7½") square (see pattern).
Divide this square into two triangles along the diagonal. Only
one of these triangles is embroidered in trapunto. The plain
side is not corded but simply *sewn* in running stitch. When
you wash your work, this section will crease gently, giving it
a pretty crinkled effect.

Wild oats

Tea cosy

This tea cosy complements the afternoon tea napkin; together they make a delightful double for any trousseau. The gentle motif is like a breath of wind in the wild oat grasses of summer.

Method

Only the front of this tea cosy is worked in the pattern. The back is simply worked in parallel lines on the diagonal.

When you've finished both sections, join the front to the back, right sides together, in machine stitching, 8 mm (⁵/₁₆″) from the edges of the work. Turn inside out, flatten the seam with your fingernail and hide the first seam within a second, to give the effect of piping. Pass 4 lengths of cotton yarn through this space.

Finally, cover the seam with a white cotton bias strip.

PATTERN (see pattern sheet)

White columbines

Baby's bib

Gifts to newborn babies are always very welcome, and provide at least as much pleasure to the person who gives them as to the child who receives them. And as you so lovingly trace these immaculate floral patterns with the point of your embroidery needle, you can imagine the cheeky, roguish little face of the baby, its smile an ample reward for your work.

Method

The parallel lines are worked at 90°, diverging from a central axis. This line divides your initial rectangle in half, and doesn't need to be sewn; it's only a guide to help you mark out 5 mm ($^3/_{16}$″) intervals for the cording.

Finish the edge of the bib with a bias strip of white satin. Make another satin bias strip for the ribbon to tie the bib around the baby's neck.

1/2 pattern
ACTUAL SIZE

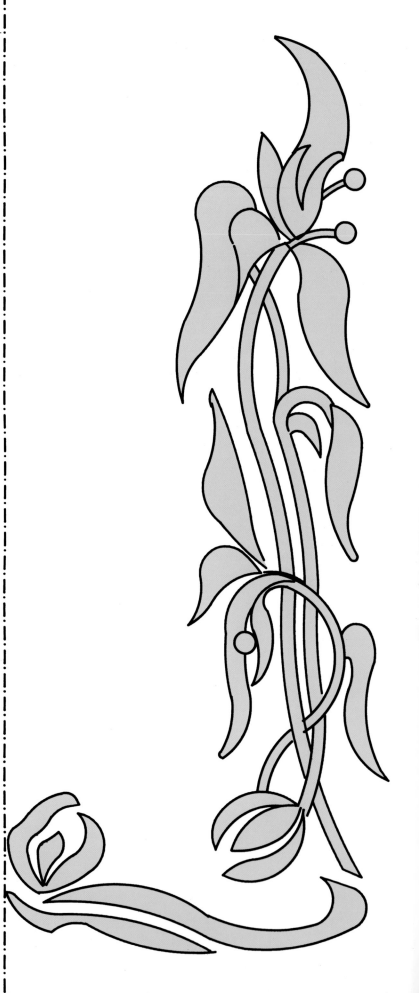

Linen tray cloth

*L*et yourself fall under the charm of the past with the old-fashioned flavour of this basket of flowers. Imagine these blooms nestled in the lap of a beautiful girl drowsing in a swing under blossoming apple trees.

Making up this piece presents little difficulty. The criss-crossed canes of the basket are filled with eight strands of the yarn used for the parallel lines.

ENLARGE AT
141%

Puff of wind

Linen tray cloth

This composition carries as its motif a lovely floral decoration done in Art Nouveau style, the long flexible leaves of the wheat rippling under the influence of a summer breeze. The central section of the tray cloth is done in extremely fine cording, using only a single thread of yarn. This light effect contrasts with the four geometric corner triangles which are corded with a doubled thread.

ENLARGE AT 200%

Tree of life

Tray cloth

Stretching its branches towards the heavens, this tree of life is a hymn to nature. Its branches are loaded with fresh flowers and the promise of fruit, and hidden within its breast lies the secret flower of knowledge.

The central cording, worked parallel to the direction of the arboreal motif, accentuates the upward movement of the tree's skyward-reaching branches.

ENLARGE AT 200%

*A*fashionable accessory in any woman's wardrobe, this piece of clothing that we have appropriated from the men has become indispensable. Here are three of them, styled in a classic shape, worked in trapunto and quilting. They are remarkable for their simple elegance.

Method

The vest is made up of three sections: the left front (photo 1), the right front (photo 2), and the back (photo 4).

The fronts are each made in two pieces (see diagram), assembled a-a' to b-b' following the diagram and stitched together with a run and fell seam along the curve of the chest. **Only the right front of the vest is worked in French trapunto**, following the technique explained on pages 6–11. Enlarge the dimensions of the two pieces making up the right front by 1 cm ($^3/_8$″) all round to allow for shrinkage from wadding and washing.

On the left front, criss-cross each piece on the diagonal with fine washaway pencil lines. Lay each piece over a fairly fine flannel of the same dimensions, then a second layer of cotton fabric, and quilt the three layers with running stitch in a fine thread which matches the fabric. Make these stitches as small and as regular as possible. Join the pieces together (a-a', b-b').

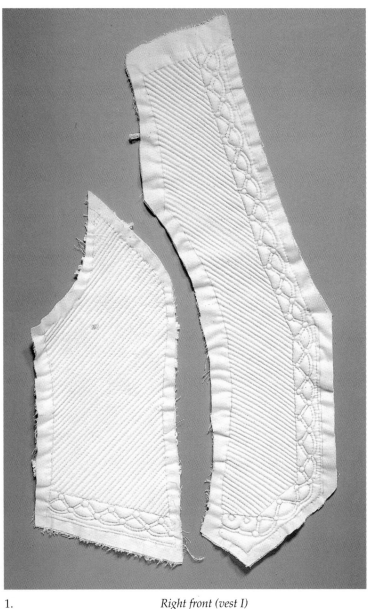

1.   *Right front (vest I)*

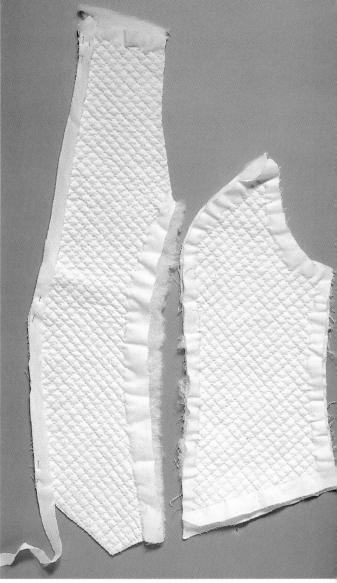

2.   *Left front (vests I, II, III)*

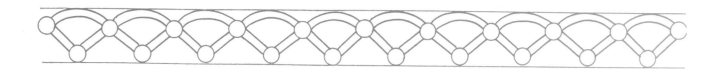

The back is made from the fine cotton fabric, lined with the same material but not quilted or decorated in any way. Remember to add the darts for shaping.

Assembling

Firstly sew the seams along the shoulders, putting together the back and the fronts of the vest using a run and fell seam. This seam is made up of a running stitch, then a hemming stitch on the underneath fabric which has been trimmed approximately 2 mm ($1/16$") from the first seam (see diagram on page 9).

Repeat for the armholes. For the edges of the front sections, cut the underneath fabric 2 mm ($1/16$") from the edge of the cording or the quilting. Fold back the lower fabric on the reverse side and sew in with tiny invisible slip stitches.

You can leave the front of the vest open, or you might choose to finish it with buttons. Sew six buttonhole loops made from the vest fabric to the right side, and add six self-covered buttons to the left side.

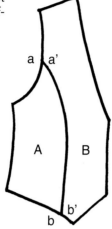

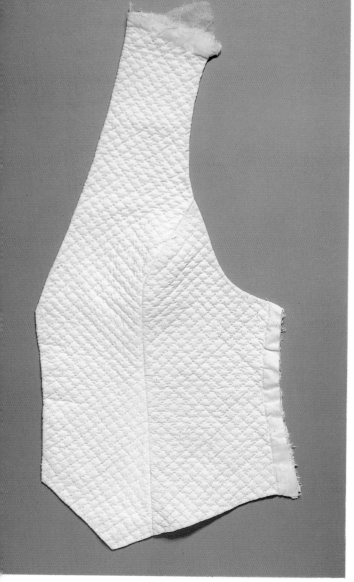

Left front assembled

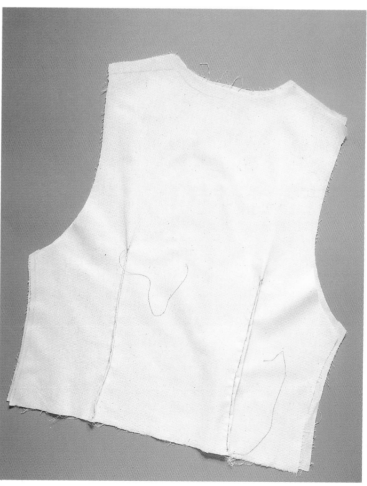

4.

Back assembled

Pas de deux

Vest I

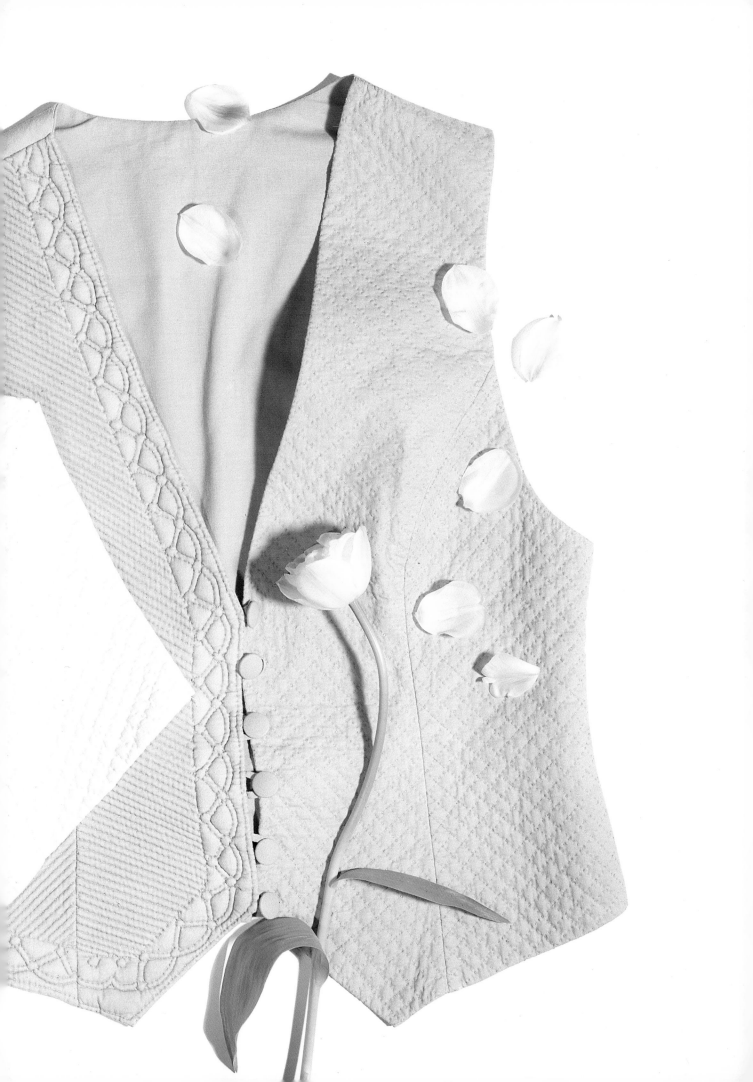

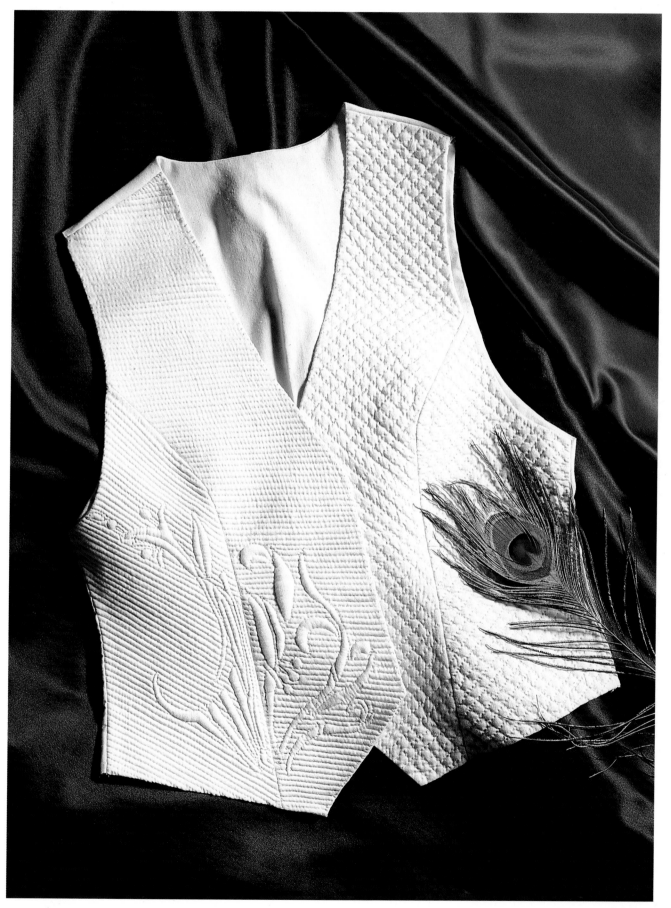

La guedra

Oriental belt

his large belt was inspired by those which you can buy at the souks in Marrakesh. Play out the fantasy and tie this simple, yet refined work nonchalantly against a coloured blouse.

The edges of the belt are finished off with a run and fell seam on the reverse of the last row of cording (see page 9).

To finish, sew a 40 cm (16") length of twisted silk cord at each end of the belt (available from furnishing and haberdashery shops), first soaking the ends in clear nail polish to prevent fraying. Alternatively, make two ties from the belt fabric. *See pattern sheet.*

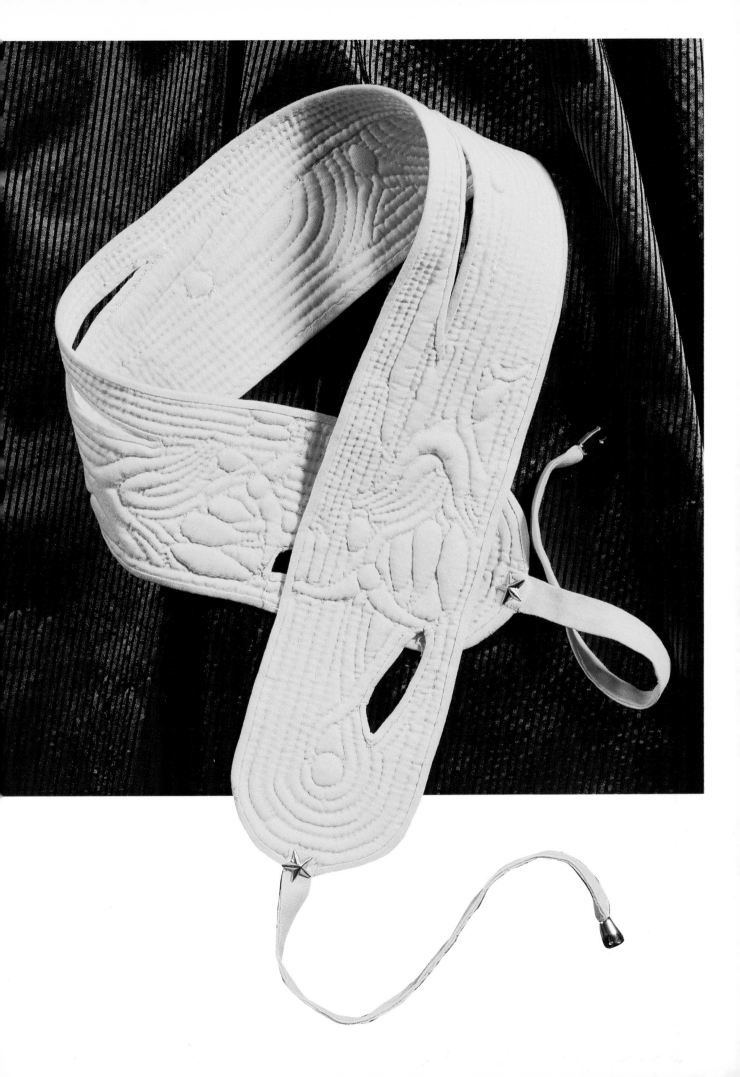

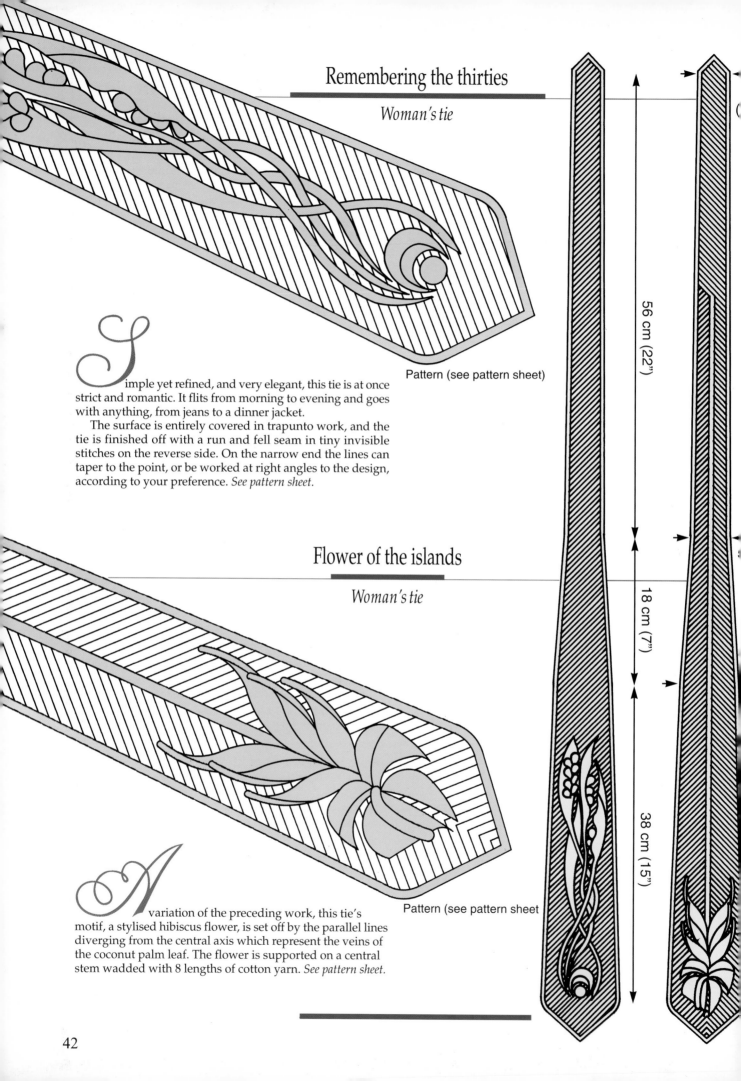

Remembering the thirties

Woman's tie

Pattern (see pattern sheet)

*S*imple yet refined, and very elegant, this tie is at once strict and romantic. It flits from morning to evening and goes with anything, from jeans to a dinner jacket.

The surface is entirely covered in trapunto work, and the tie is finished off with a run and fell seam in tiny invisible stitches on the reverse side. On the narrow end the lines can taper to the point, or be worked at right angles to the design, according to your preference. *See pattern sheet.*

Flower of the islands

Woman's tie

Pattern (see pattern sheet

A variation of the preceding work, this tie's motif, a stylised hibiscus flower, is set off by the parallel lines diverging from the central axis which represent the veins of the coconut palm leaf. The flower is supported on a central stem wadded with 8 lengths of cotton yarn. *See pattern sheet.*

56 cm (22")

18 cm (7")

38 cm (15")

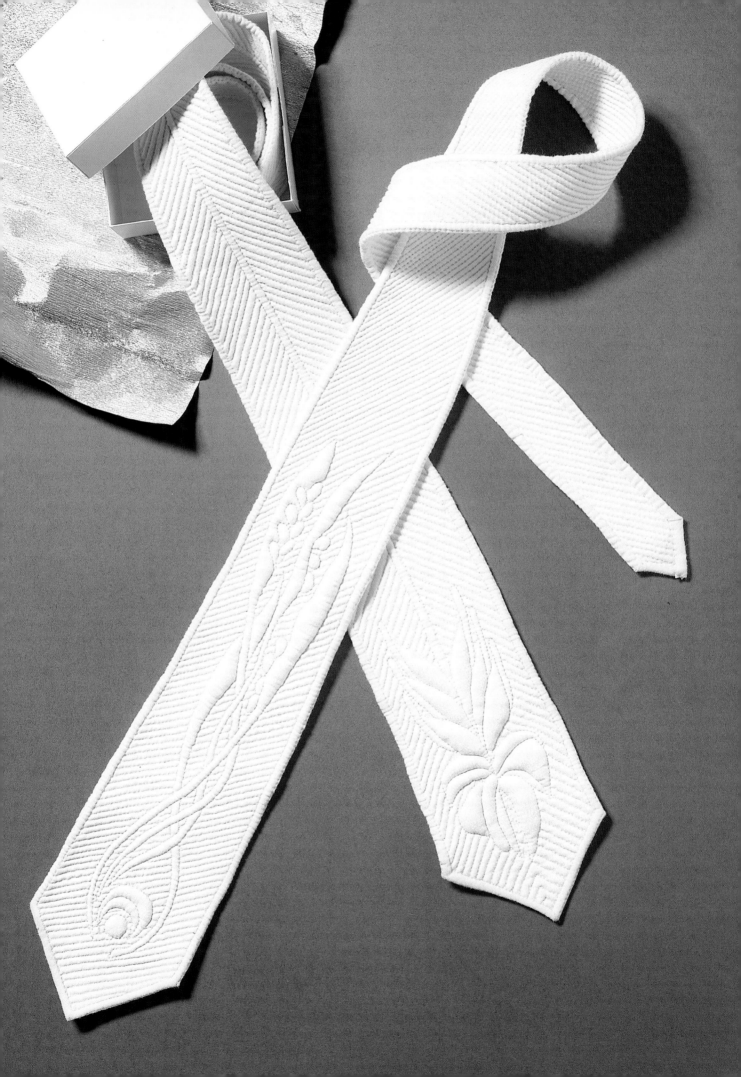

Cotton flower

A tiny object of irresistible charm, straight out of grandmother's sewing box, this needlecase will be like a jewellery case for your more precious needles—those which are gilded around the eye of the needle, making the point seem even finer.

Method

Make up a sort of small book of fabrics, a rectangle divided into two crosswise.

The right side, which is the front of the needlecase, is worked in trapunto, while the left side (the back), is simply stitched with random small stitches over the surface and not stuffed. Washing will cause this section to bunch up and create a pretty crinkled effect. All four edges are trimmed with a row of cording.

For the needle pages, cut four rectangles of white fabric, making them 5 mm (³/₁₆") smaller than the cover all around.

Sew two pieces together, right sides facing. Turn inside out and finish sewing by hand, with tiny slip stitches. Repeat with the other two pieces. Lay them together and fold them in half. Place the fold in the exact centre and sew in place with a line of backstitching. Don't go through the outer layer, so that the stitching remains invisible from the outside.

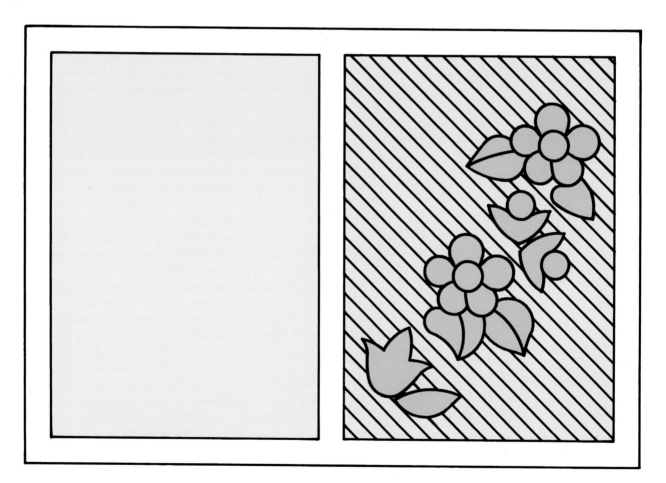

ACTUAL SIZE

A as in 'affection', 'amuse-
ment', 'adventure', or simply A as the first
letter of the alphabet. A trapunto
alphabet is something you could
perhaps design for yourself.

Contents